PIER

PIER

Janine Oshiro

ALICE JAMES BOOKS
FARMINGTON, MAINE

10 9 8 7 6 5 4 3 2 1

Alice James Books are published by Alice James Poetry Cooperative, Inc.,
an affiliate of the University of Maine at Farmington.

ALICE JAMES BOOKS
238 MAIN STREET
FARMINGTON, ME 04938

www.alicejamesbooks.org

Library of Congress Cataloging-in-Publication Data

Oshiro, Janine.
    Pier / Janine Oshiro.
    p. cm.
    Poems.
    ISBN 978-1-882295-88-3
    I. Title.
PS3615.S45P54 2011
811'.6--dc22
    2011015819

Alice James Books gratefully acknowledges support from individual donors, private foundations, the
University of Maine at Farmington and the National Endowment for the Arts. ❦

Cover art:
Alastair Magnaldo, "La jetée"
www.almagnus.com

CONTENTS

Wake

Acknowledgments

My warm thanks to the editors and staff of the following publications in which some of these poems first appeared, sometimes in different forms:

Bamboo Ridge: "Intermission," "Setting," and "Mountain Vision"
Beloit Poetry Journal: "Next,Dust"
Caffeine Destiny: "Pavilion Vision" and "Ecstatic Vision"
Colorado Review: "Chorus"
Greatcoat: "Duck Hunting" and "Habitat"
Kaimana: Literary Arts Hawai'i: "In the Beginning" and "February"
Propeller: "Move" and "Snow Logic"
Thermos: "Praise," "Rest," "Invitation," and "Anniversary"

Thank you to Literary Arts in Oregon for supporting me with a fellowship in 2004. Thank you to the University of Iowa for a Dean's Graduate Merit Fellowship, which afforded me unencumbered time to complete this collection.

To Sarah Gambito, Joseph O. Legaspi, Jennifer Chang, Vikas Menon, and my Kundiman fellows, I offer my deepest gratitude for creating a stimulating and supportive space for Asian-American poets.

Sincere thanks to my teachers at Whitworth University, Portland State University, and the University of Iowa, especially Laurie Lamon and Michele Glazer. Thank you to my workshop friends from Portland State University and the University of Iowa for inspiring me with your own work.

I offer my love and gratitude to my family and friends in Hawai'i and Portland. To Shanda Tice, my dear friend, thank you for insisting that I partake in all the goodness the world has to offer: such joy and abundance.

For Richard, Keith, and Troy Oshiro

Earth's the right place for love:
I don't know where it's likely to go better.
—Robert Frost

Habitat

Nor do I want to lie down
in this pond,

reflecting the eye, reflecting
the pond until the first

frog jumps.
I iterate, I

iterate.
Little frog, come to me

greenly. Come open
your sometimes flappable throat,

elastic, make room for the high notes.
I want to turn you supposedly

inside out like a pocket.
It is evening out: one side

drift, one side waste.
Tears are surplus

in such a watery place.
The stones around the pond

display the shapeliness of a wide
collar, an invitation.

So I shall begin by striking small
hammers in the ear. It was

morning, yes, and all
the frogs were thumbnail sized.

I was in the garden, next
to the temple, yes. Inside

was something going on like a calendar
to mark the days

without.
Here is the robe (amphibian raiment).

Here is a paper house to burn.
Here are the stones that address the pond.

Now count down
the rings at the top of the temple.

The invasive frogs are said to die upon
leaving their original habitat.

A pleading look in the eyes, sun-
shined, eclipsed by

a pupil. I want outside.
In the wrist is a bone like a boat.

I have been a long time out of water.

Adrift

The times are nightfall, look, their light grows less;
The times are winter, watch, a world undone:
—Gerard Manley Hopkins

First Vision

Senior portraits are distinguished by that particular soft focus, hazy light considered *romantic*, somehow more *memorable*. "How mature she looks!" "Those eyes…" The first time I took a plane, I saw my mother's senior portrait in the clouds. So clearly did she appear, I almost asked the man beside me to confirm it. But I was leaving home and afraid he might have said, leaning over my lap and squinting, "That's *my* mother there, sitting for a portrait in the sky."

Every time after the first time
I took a plane, my mind played a child's game.

"But what do you see in the clouds?"

THREE CAPES

One
: a scenic.

Coastal pine grows in a blown position. Windswept returning
to wind, still
            pine. Kinnikinnick, commonly
bearberry, locks down the dirt.

When the tide rises, it stows away the beach past the point.
When it's low, I'm afraid of being trapped there.

Two
: a garment beyond fit,
                oceanic.

Bayocean, a plausible dream city on a spit, fell when
the currents changed.
                The hem let its water down.
One: fasten the hasp, call it home.

                        Two: run
through salty streets, yellow lawns the ocean combs, come back

for one:
        a finger cut off from land.

Who knew which way was pointing?

Three
: the toy train no longer makes its circuit.

In the mural of the coast, at Rachel's Family Dining on the coast,
curved lines one way mean waves, birds
                                                        the other.
A boy won't stop saying, "A crack in the track, a crack in the track

a crack…" Latch
                        a line around each thing and make it so,
a buoyant tail, a splash, the grooves along a whale's body.

One: the owner built a ledge to run a train along the wall.
One: my neck struck cold by my mother at the empty table.
One: I return for the empty table.
One: I return for

Three

SPIT

Spit is a narrow strip of land extending into water. *Strip* means the disrobing of the outer layer, while *spit* may suggest a piercing through the center. One may strip a spit of its contents, or spit to force what's inside to come out. Thus, one may say that *spit* resides in *strip*, but *spit* will likely find its way out. *Spit* may be spilt from the corner of the mouth or, more likely, slip intact from the bottom lip. *Spindrift* is the sea's spittle. Perhaps the magnification of what is released from a whale's spiracle. Water suspends in air; fine particles of sand suspend in water; water deposits the sand as silt back on land. One supposes that a spit composed of silt will quickly slip away. Or cause fits of choking. A *slip* is a narrow space between piers for docking ships. Or a fine women's garment. When she came to me, she wore a slip of silt [*sic*]. *Spiculate* describes the starfish.

Next, Dust

As opposed to mineral, usually cold, as opposed to hot, I woke to the *zip zip zip zip* of it, in the shape of a square, in the surface of the wall, what an architect might call the skin of the building. The sound was higher around the corners, because tighter, and what came out, from inside the skin, made no other sound.

Who said the wall was flat didn't know the insides of it.
Who said the ghost was inside flayed the body to determine its
    position.

She, a house in a house, removed from the wall, was, herself, full. Was she asleep when it moved upon her? She was not dreaming. She said, my body, a ruined machine, upon which what moves makes me into another.

It moved *up-on* me.

I felt the feet first   on my head because on my head   and cold
        then it ran   down me   my body a plank
by that time hot   as opposed to mineral   I was inside

and feet were running the length of me and how far

The skin and brain in the embryo are formed from the same membrane. We think upon this surface, we feel upon this selfsame house. Without our skin we would not recognize the order of disbelief, or the recurrence of figs and slips of paper, each one with a different meaning,

or the white handkerchief, ironed and flat.

I believe I am myself
in relation to: rock candy
         small feet
         impossible tasks.

When it happened
I didn't know the word for it.

My mother's skin—starched—a sheet-
like organ, unflappable by the wind.
Her skin became hard.

The presentation is commonly distal to proximal. It begins in the fingertips and proceeds up the arm. Creation begins here, in the scar tissue, which hardens. There are words and there are words: God's fingertip bringing a girl into being.

(I wrapped my arms
around her, threw my leg over
her when we slept.)

By the time the upper arms have hardened, there may be stiffness in the legs or abdomen.

(Sometimes I fell asleep next
to her and woke with my arms wrapped
around a rolled up blanket.)

Or the insides may turn to stone,

next, dust.

The skin of the face and neck may also be involved. The skin may appear red and shiny. Polished fruit. Finger tightness. The problem may be a gold wreck on the outside. There may be happiness. There may be a fantasy of hollow skin.

For example, the wall.

Touch is the first of the senses to develop in the womb.

There are places on the back where
we are unable to perceive the difference
between two small feet an inch apart

and the prick of a single point.

I think she is a certain wonder.

In the hospital room was not a ghost, but her body, eyelids taped shut. I did not ask how she would see to find her way back to our house. White tape, neither transparent nor opaque, kept the windows shut. I believed in windows. I believed in her insides, as if her body were a basket or a hurdle to leap over. My body, this temple. How she would disperse.

Meaning without the word.

She knocked on the door.
The door was hard.

She knocked without her hand.
(She was dead.)

I knew better than to let her in.
She came in.

My mouth opened to answer her
questions unheard, questions unknown

unlike the door
(locked)

the carpet
(yellow)

the ceiling
(high beamed

and knotted).

Everywhere is a potential
exit, except the door.

I drew a high wall at the skin;
at the bottom I drew a gutter.

I was eleven.
These are the words I have for it.

RELIC

Enter the slender
room between the rooms
used mainly to hang
the pictures. Hang
her picture with tacks.
Look to both ends of
the room to stay
impermanence. Remember
(will you remember?)
the color reserved
under her picture around
which the sun sets.
An astonishing number of
harmful things can happen
to objects made out
of paper: foxing,
excreta of insects,
lux—that is to say,
our bodies rust.
It may be hard to make
the sound of words: *tack, tack*.
But make the mishap.
There is a crease settling in
the chamber of your throat.

Rest

That white place is without ghost.
Having been there once, I want to return
to violets,

part through their umbrella clump
of leaves
as my hands divide from prayer.

In the white place I tried
to draw a horizon.
I wanted days, minutes, a distance to seek,

a resting place
for the sun to mark the time. But the horizon was
all wrong.

It came out in a child's hand and I was
not a child.
I had been waiting

in a hallway before the white place.
I was not alone.
I had been waiting for my mother and she came.

I kept the time by her going.
I prayed for her return and I prayed for her
return to the dead.

The hallway had walls, a floor
to kneel on.
In the white place I was alone.

Without even her, without
even ground
to pull the stems from.

Tack

... sanctuary, sanctuary, *I say it over and over and the*
word's sound is the one place to dwell: that's it, just
the sound, and the imagination of the sound—a place.

—A.R. Ammons

ANNIVERSARY

I fashioned an acre, made moderate
the interior.
Pinned in the crickets with their decent clicking.
At the end of July appeared one animal.

I mustered up a mountain for a view.
The opposing houses shone like
straightened teeth.
They were two-storied,

the second ones forthcoming.
At the top of each staircase the door was unlocked.
Inside each house lived one
obedient daughter.

I put the daughter there I put the daughter there.
Not a window cracked its milky
reflection of the clouds.
The glass bowls on the shelves were nested.

I expected the animal to introduce
the next disaster. Its mouth was a cushioned entry otherwise
unpronounced its abundant legs rambled proposing
no use.

I kept an eye on the animal and nothing happened.
The mountain blistered and popped into its plural.
I kept an eye on the animal.
The sky remained where it was, distant.

The obedient daughters kept their houses neat.
The animal remained the animal except
with ears alert, unrecognizable.
(*Sing*) My eyes leaked spilly spilly all the way home.

Duck Hunting

Find another way in.

Sometimes cutting a hole and falling in is the only way to go.
Once,

it is an illusion. A list in the dark is one side of her face. It is dark
in my ordinary vision. It is almost so plain

it's a statement.

Her arms hang down so low you might think she is an animal. Like-
wise the cow in the marsh. This is where water and land combine to
make *wetlands*. The cow's body appears above its head, but it is not
upside down. Once,

it was an illusion.

Come backache, come rapture, come reconfigure
sky. Come watch the show of her knees in the grass.

For this formal occasion, accumulate detail, carouse sound. Tell her to put on her red bathing suit and stand in the painting. For this formal occasion, a boat stuck in the mud. And to account for this distortion, the frame

to confer an awkward end.
See skin: shiny, milked, a cold coming.

She wore it well.

Narrate the lesson in the bathing suit. Say it. *How do I be inside of me?* Be careful when you raise your arms above your head. Be careful of the house beyond the trees.

Or cow tight cow low a funny fragrance.

And how she is looking past the main attraction!
A duck like a firework.

The hunter, he lives in the house beyond the trees. He lives in that corner. Believe me. It is dark, and darkly

seen, the duck is falling.

PRAISE

Heaven is a prop that the stage-
hands erect on stage before
my brother and sister descend
from it to invent the world.
My brother and sister existed
before the world. They brush off
praise for eyelashes and cuticles
and look away when I say,
my brother, my sister.
Who am I to say *my brother?*
Who am I to say *my sister?*
The stagehands' bodies dressed
in black appear seamless against
the dark curtain. The hands
that draw the curtain shut open it
with the same mechanical button.
My brother, my sister, I am clapping
my hands to welcome you to invent
the world I am dying to enter.

INTERMISSION

In a performance of peeing
outdoors, my uncle came out
from the cane fields as if
from behind a curtained fringe
of sunlit green. "Girl"
—he called me girl then, when
I was one, now girl
that I am past one—
"Say excuse me, girl,
before you go in these fields.
You never know what came
before, you never
know who's there."

Pavilion Vision

Maybe causal, it was casual—
it happened at a fair.
People bustled under
lights strung blinking in
the afternoon. Before I was
stolen and kept in this room
whose walls are paper
screen doors, I was watching
the dancing man in the pavilion.
Wrapped up in robes and knotted
sashes, he loosed his hands
to flutter. How his face glowed
an orange-red lantern! Skin is
fixative to light, and powder—
how does it compensate?

The doors replay the shadows
of the fair until his visit.
Little whisk of steps.
I say he is a woman in how
his hands move like white blossoms.
I take the branch
and shake it. What happens next, it
is said, is like the rain.

ELEVEN DANCERS

The dancers' legs are cut off.
Stage set for the dancing
blockade—black—like their legs.

They could be amputees. Darkness
where legs used to be.
White suits hover.

Clearly, innocuous as a checkered floor.

Stutter of hips, the smallest twitch
to startle the loudest sneeze!
Torsos contract, spines

releasing order. Letting the heads go.
Description fits.
The dancers dance in black and white.

huhúh   huhúh

AUDIENCE

Curtain call: center stage,
there sits a row of chairs.

Legs lined up so from
the side they might seem one.

The lighting makes their high backs something
to applaud.

Act one: The Chairs Are Empty
Act two: The Chairs Misspeak The Line of The Elbow
Act three: Reside Among the Rest of Them
Act four:

There is one with a guest in her spine.

I write and rewrite my review.

"They [the chairs] made a courage of waiting."

CONSPICITURSUS

A bear catches sight of a sow it is said it is seen

Seeing is believing except when it comes to bears

Except when it comes to bears bells signal welcome

If a bear appears sing a song

Repeat the chorus

A song about a bear usually has an upbeat

Rhythm itself is a pleasure

Sing the song about the sow with the see-through stomach

It will make yours ache

Unbearable is the sound of the sow in trouble

The song remains

Unseen a bear or a sow is rustling the leaves behind you

ECSTATIC VISION

The sound she made me make, it was
a what-
aphant. My voice

woke me to a girl
standing beside me.
She came to find and found what
in the room I could not see.
But the bed was bigger than I recalled
and the thing keeping
down my chest would not
let go. *Let me go.*

She would not let up
her stare.

Her hair was cut just
below her chin. She stood in
the bathroom's light
and stared at it

on top of me, a
whataphant awaking.

Snow Logic

In the world of telling, it is
said that where the snow
rushes the earth, the bears are white.
My empty bowl is in
the world of telling. Spoon,
unfinished state of being
a moon, my only handle.
If in my empty bowl should live
a bear, what color would reflect
in his dark eyes?

Certainly, my empty bowl
is white. Certainly,
the bear would look like snow.
The weather report goes
a long way to strip
the color from his eyes.
Snow sparks and flaws
his vision. The gusts pick up
and carry me his growl
as a squeaky falsetto.

Before I saw snow, I saw
pictures of snow and believed
in it. And so of bears.
Snow blinded I am. A bear
is nothing like its picture.
Look up, look up.
Bear, interrupt
my empty bowl of reason.
Show me that the end
I know is wrong.

Wake

For there is a boundary to looking.
And the world that is looked at so deeply
wants to flourish in love.

—Rainer Maria Rilke

Mountain Vision

Because vision is a sign of so much, as a kind of test for which the only result is failure or great imagination, I look to the mountain and say that I can see him. I know what the mountain is called. His head rests in one place, his feet in another, his face a sudden cliff where birds might land and never wonder about the landscape's correspondence to a chin. My sleeping giant reclines halfway across the island, his lumpy stomach shook up with wind, his feet a clever fit of boulders. What would it mean to be bigger than this fine idea of resemblance? On the pleasant hike atop his body, I make in the light some kind of bird with my hands where his nose comes to peak. Call me remiss—I want to call the ambiguous mountain, *mountain.* Deny the palms look like lashes.

In the Beginning

I do not want it
to belong to me, nor do
I want it to belong to you.
Sing me any song
except the one that spells
the singing alphabet. (It
makes no sense, making sense
even in reverse.)
I will sing too.
Are you happy and/or sad?
Are you alone and/or not alone?
Of the many ways of
being lonely, I'll take the one
that happens when I have nothing
at all to say and you are
listening. Nearby flows
the Cedar River, named for the trees
(of the juniper, not the cedar, genus)
that grow along
its palisades. A palisade
is something like a rock fence
along the river that the river
did not form. Or
something that could pierce
a heart. The river begins
near Blooming Prairie, which I know
not as an actual place—as in, once
when I was in Blooming Prairie—but as I know my noisy birth,
(I am telling you now about the beginning)
and as I know
my grandma's amputated leg

has become home
to the oldest ant
who ever lived, who lived
in a laboratory to be
twenty-nine years old.

INVITATION

Having not seen it
happen but knowing
it happened

a black snake
crawled down my spine.
Something but what is

wrong. I make my desire
for the rain to stop visible
by stacking three flat

stones. I make my desire for you
not a marker of direction.
I never saw

the wasps alive. I
never saw them fall but the floor
of my house is

covered with them. Because
asking is kin
to knowing. Please

will you reach
your hand into my back?
Get it out.

SETTING

I stalk the spoons

from shore. They cut

through waves as nowhere

else. Schools

of blunt tips,

their tenuous hollows caught

by the finishing

light. I lure

them with dough I pop

from cans. Breakable,

I am generous, but they

resist the holding instinct.

They cannot bite.

Neither can I net.

Nor gut their silver out.

They swivel as
they swim, the big ones

breaking the surface like

drills. The small

ones peek their tops

out in a row of winking

sunsets. Stranded,

I am without

the proper utensil.

The shore spools on and

off my ankles.

Move

On the first day, the sea
squirt swims until finding
a place of attachment.

When the woman smiles at me, I mouth
the words, "I'm sorry." My father's piss
hits the creeping sheet of water flooding
the street in front of her house.
His elastic legs can point in every direction.
His stream hits the surface then deflects into an arc
that falls back down into his open mouth.

When the woman smiles at me, I know she means
how difficult it is to love.

On the first day, the sea squirt swims until finding a place
of attachment.

+

I wish, I wish not to discuss
these places that prong up.

My inside's flower won't.
The petals splay and out comes.

On the first day, the sea.

+

To cleanse the organs, make your fist
into an external one. Punch it into your stomach
and double over as if in pain. Stay doubled,

release. Now
if you cut it off, can you
serve it on a platter?

Hand, say wing.
Hand, say fight.
Hand, take flight to keep the water flowing.

An extra finger, my father
pokes a needle into himself to flush
out all the waste.
He wants me to see him drain it out.
He turns on the faucet of his belly.

+

On the first
day the sea
squirt swims
until finding
a place of a-
ttachment

When people say my name, I think they mean
me, but they may have someone else in mind.
At the Waikiki Aquarium, I watch the frogfish
all day. Brown and still like a piece of shit
anchored to the bottom of the tank.

The sign says the frogfish looks like a little man.
I look like my father. I reply to his face.

then, having no reason to move, the sea squirt eats
its brain and tail.

+

On the first day, the end of the first day.

If attached, a pest; if of the open
sea,

pelagic.
I love him.

This is the end of the pier,
where I am only one of many well-
wishers.

See how the piles root in two directions?

When the boat pulls out
automatically
I wave when waved to from the deck.

FEBRUARY

I went to the river to make
myself feel better on the second
day of the midwinter thaw.
I wanted to stand on the floating
dock to feel something,
I thought, dangerous as if
its stays—frozen over—
could have split, and broken
off I could have drifted
down like ice. But
the dock stayed, only partially
iced in, a rim of water
gathering dull white fish
at the surface. Underneath
the still surface water
water kept a quicker flow.
Along the river bank
sloped spilling snow
and ice that seeped into
the exhausted suck of grass.

The willow shined.
Each hanging whip adorned
with hardened buds that clung
like talons. Beneath it,
half in water, half
on ice, a goose had made
or found an icy crevice
for its body. Its feathers stood
out oddly at a ruffle, almost
tucked in. At first
I thought it was falling

asleep, its limp neck
curling down and sliding on
the ice. Its neck
jerked up, it shook, it bent
its neck. I watched
it ribbon down and stiffen
up. I watched it ribbon
down. It was not spring.

Chorus

Said of him slow
the man I
see at death
unlike any spring
river seen
        I am
the slow man's gait
slow of the slow
man's handshake
when we meet

So said river come
to rise and swell
the bark
      soak up
the dates inked in
the rings of trees
once planted neatly
in a row of three
now growing in
the widened river

Said bark or
flower as wind
sifts through
the autumn
leaves still clung
to not yet
spring so said
the song that empties
me out
when I sing to him

I said it is so
I love the smiling
man whose name
I don't know
smiling at death

           one

smiling at death

           two

I keep the count
down

Expect the saying
death will come
in three
   so clap
your hands
     one two
to enter prayer
       don't bow at the neck
bend at the waist and
naturally

Said so naturally
of seasons
            the river rose
slow bend
before unseen
                the outcome
pouring one
current into another
into days I'm still
counting

Said of him a second
hand defying
its internal
mechanism's ticking
ticking
   a blur
the hand released
to gravity hanging
below the set
numerical face

So said I
I am his
I am his
slow smiling
face face
I lift my hands
to bless before
I blow away
at night as
white ashes

Notes

"Spit" is after an 1863 diary entry by Gerard Manley Hopkins.

"Next, Dust" borrows language from medical texts about scleroderma.

"Duck Hunting" is after the painting of the same name by Oskar Kokoschka, and it is for John Craun.

"Conspicitursus" takes its title from mention of the two possibilities of meaning in a manuscript without spacing—conspicit ursus (a bear espies) and conspicitur sus (a sow is espied)—in *Pause and Effect: Punctuation in the West* by M.B. Parkes.

"In the Beginning" is for Melissa Dickey and Sam Reed.

Book Benefactors

Alice James Books and Janine Oshiro wish to thank the following
individuals, who generously contributed toward the publication of
Pier:
Cynthia King

For more information about AJB's book benefactor program,
contact us via phone or email, or visit us at www.alicejamesbooks.org
to see a list of forthcoming titles.

The Kundiman Poetry Prize was founded in 2010 and is an annual book publication prize open to emerging and established poets of Asian American descent. The prize is offered through partnership between Alice James Books and Kundiman, a nonprofit organization devoted to the preservation and promotion of Asian American poetry. In addition to book publication and $1000, awarded by Alice James Books, the recipient of The Kundiman Poetry Prize receives a Kundiman-sponsored featured reading.

Winners of The Kundiman Poetry Prize:

2010, Janine Oshiro, *Pier*

Recent Titles from Alice James Books

Alice James Books has been publishing poetry since 1973
and remains one of the few presses in the country that is run collectively.
The cooperative selects manuscripts for publication primarily
through regional and national annual competitions. Authors who win a
Kinereth Gensler Award become active members of the cooperative
board and participate in the editorial decisions of the press. The press,
which historically has placed an emphasis on publishing women poets,
was named for Alice James, sister of William and Henry, whose fine
journal and gift for writing went unrecognized during her lifetime.

Typeset and Designed by
Pamela A. Consolazio

Printed by Thomson-Shore
on 30% postconsumer recycled paper
processed chlorine-free